A souvenir guide

Alfriston Clergy House
East Sussex

Anthony Lambert

C000262969

National Trust

Blueprint for a
National Endeavour

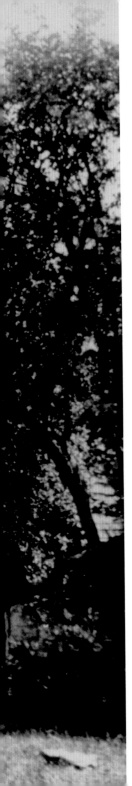

Few buildings in Britain can rival Alfriston Clergy House for its place in the story of architectural conservation. Had the attempt to save it failed, the fate of many other fine buildings in need of rescue would have been in jeopardy.

Thanks to the determination of a Sussex clergyman, the faith and generosity of a few dozen people and the courage of the National Trust's founders, the Wealden hall-house known as the Clergy House became the infant charity's first building, which it saved and restored by the skin of its teeth.

The Rev. Beynon's campaign

The idea of saving the Clergy House came from the Rev. Frederick William Beynon who became vicar of Alfriston in 1889, by which time the house was virtually derelict. It had not been occupied since the death of Harriet Coates in 1883, who had wished to end her days there despite its decrepit condition, and permission to demolish it had been given by the Ecclesiastical Commissioners.

Beynon had demonstrated his love of old buildings while a curate in Yorkshire, converting an old barn into a Mission Church near Denaby Main Colliery in the 1870s, along with setting up 'Night Schools, Mothers' Meeting, and the opening of a Reading Room, with its various classes for instruction and amusement…' The Clergy House must have seemed ripe for similar use.

For advice Beynon turned to the Sussex Archaeological Society and then to the Society for the Protection of Ancient Buildings (SPAB).

In 1893 he published an appeal for the 'Alfriston Old Clergy House Preservation Fund', having secured the names of the dukes of Norfolk, Devonshire and Newcastle as well as deans and bishops to add weight to the appeal.

In 1890 Beynon had commissioned Owen Fleming, an architect with London County Council, to examine the building and produce costed recommendations. Fleming estimated the work would require £447, less £100 if a minstrels' gallery in his plan was omitted. To staunch the rain, a roof of matchboarding was put up in 1893, but the following year Fleming withdrew under pressure of other work and Beynon commissioned another survey, from the London brewery architect Henry Stock.

Beynon received nothing but discouragement locally, and he later wrote rather bitterly in the *Daily Chronicle* that 'not a shilling has been given inside the parish to preserve the building, whilst Noah when building his ark could scarcely have been subjected to more open scorn and silent contempt for what was regarded as my hobby and my folly.'

By 1894 it must have become evident to Beynon that more help was needed, and in July the SPAB advised him to contact the National Trust whose Provisional Council agreed on 16 July to procure the charity's legal incorporation.

'…a man of untiring energy, and devotion to work…'

In an illuminated address to the Rev. Beynon signed by 412 colliers and their wives from Denaby Main Colliery when he left the parsonage at Denaby, 1876

Opposite The state of the Clergy House must have seemed daunting to the National Trust's founders, all novices when it came to the restoration of historic buildings. Sadly the identity of the people around the entrance door has been lost

Saved by the National Trust

The Clergy House was just the sort of building within the sights of the embryonic National Trust; the notion of anything as large as a country house was simply unthinkable. Yet not everyone on the Provisional Committee agreed with the proposal to buy it.

The architect Alfred Waterhouse strongly opposed it on the grounds of cost, but Octavia Hill thought 'the same spirit which had saved Parliament Hill would save many a lovely view or old ruin or manor house from destruction and for the everlasting delight of thousands of people of these islands.'

Though Octavia Hill was passionate about 'open air sitting rooms for the poor', her experience in the renovation of slum property made it natural for her to take charge of repairs at Alfriston. Nothing could be done until ownership was secured, and her frustration with the legal niceties is palpable in her letters, but on 16 April 1896 the Trust's Chairman Sir Robert Hunter and the Honorary Secretary Canon Hardwicke Rawnsley signed the conveyance. The National Trust had acquired its first building, for £10.

The thinking in March 1896 was to install a caretaker at one end and to open the rest to visitors who 'might have tea', Octavia Hill thought, rather presciently, 'or which might possibly, under proper supervision, be available for some parish purposes.'

Left Sir Robert Hunter (1844–1913) was already a veteran campaigner through his work as solicitor to the Commons Preservation Society when he conceived the idea of a 'National Trust'. He became its architect and first Chairman

Below left Canon Hardwicke Rawnsley (1851–1920) was the vicar of Crosthwaite near Keswick when he became the National Trust's first Secretary. His former headmaster thought him 'so far from commonplace, so original, so full of strange power, that I find it impossible to form the same kind of absolute judgement on his future that I could do in less exceptional cases, but I have every confidence that the outcome will be good'. He was an ardent campaigner against the despoliation of the Lake District fells which he loved

Opposite Octavia Hill (1838–1912). Her management of properties for the Ecclesiastical Commissioners doubtless helped in the acquisition of the Clergy House since its sale required the approval of the Lord Chancellor, the Bishop of Chichester and the commissioners

It was a struggle raising enough money to restore the building: in March 1897 Octavia Hill wrote to Rawnsley that 'nothing comes in for it … We <u>can</u> hold our hand, but it seems a pity. All my friends seem keener about beautiful open space … We don't seem to reach the antiquaries & artists.'

Though secondary to success in saving the Clergy House, the approach taken to its restoration was a formative influence in the Trust's subsequent work. The SPAB became involved in the choice of someone to undertake the restoration work, in the words of Octavia Hill, 'a man … who could be there himself whose heart was in the matter and who could decide point by point on the spot what to do and see to it being done, with knowledge of art and craft seems to be essential.'

That person was Alfred Hoare Powell who had trained in the office of the church architect J.D. Sedding. Powell combined architecture with craft and design, decorating ceramics for Wedgwood and furniture made by Ernest Gimson and Sidney Barnsley. Powell acted as 'master of works' at Alfriston and estimated £250 to render the building secure and weatherproof and a further £100 for full, desirable repairs.

Octavia Hill

Octavia Hill was born in Wisbech, Cambridgeshire, in 1838, into a family noted for public service. Her childhood was spent in Finchley and Marylebone where she met John Ruskin, and it was a loan from him that enabled her to rehabilitate slum properties and take on the management of others. The preservation of open spaces became her next concern, developing her reputation as a social reformer. Ruskin also introduced her to another of the National Trust's founders, Canon Hardwicke Rawnsley.

'… the pleading voice of the old building … to tell its story to the days that are to come.'

Octavia Hill

The Building

Many two-storey 'Wealden' hall-houses were built in the Weald between the North and South Downs with money derived from sheep-farming estates and the export trade in wool through Seaford.

We do not know when or by whom the Clergy House was built on the west bank of the tidal River Cuckmere, but it was between 1370 and 1450. The typical plan of the three-bay house was simple. A central Hall open to the rafters was flanked by end chambers on each floor, the upper one jettied out at the front. At the east end were the family rooms, with a Parlour downstairs and a living room with sleeping quarters above. At the west end were humbler service rooms for domestic tasks and sleeping accommodation for the servants above. The entrance door opened into the Hall opposite a door in the rear elevation. The Hall's west wall was pierced by two doorways with ogee heads into the original service rooms.

An oak frame provides rigidity, and the spaces between are filled with wattle and daub – mud or clay and chalk with a binder such as grass or straw and water or urine, applied over a wattlework of interwoven strips of unseasoned oak and then limewashed. Though the crown-post roof is now thatched, it may once have been covered by rough, heavy Horsham stone.

In the mid-16th century the service bay was demolished and replaced by a crosswing with a tile-hung west wall and simple vertical studs instead of characteristic curved braces. The crosswing projected to the rear of the house and incorporated a new Parlour and additional room to the south with two rooms above. A bulky twin-flue brick chimneybreast with oven was built on to the west wall and a single-flue chimney built against the rear wall of the Hall, which was divided horizontally by inserting a floor with a doorway on the upper level only at the west end.

In about 1600 glazed windows replaced all or most of the openings, previously screened only by shutters. In the mid-18th century the rear bay of the crosswing was demolished to allow construction of a lean-to the full length of the south front. Finally at some time in the 18th or early 19th century the building was divided into two cottages.

Opposite The Parlour, seen through the ogee-headed doorways in the Hall's west wall

Life in a hall-house

Life revolved around the Hall and its open fire, smoke escaping through open windows, gaps in the Horsham roof tiles and possibly through a triangular gablet at the end of the ridge in the hipped roof. The floor was of rammed chalk and sour milk.

Even before the Hall was divided horizontally, cooking is likely to have migrated to the service rooms which are commonly known as the buttery, where butts of ale and wine, vessels and utensils were stored, and the pantry for storage of food, especially bread.

At the east end the family occupied the Parlour and the upper chamber known as the solar, which was used as the family's bed- and sitting-room. The 'best' end of the house was altered from east to west with the mid-16th-century reconstruction of the east end.

Above left The jettied north-east corner

Above The floor of rammed sour milk and chalk in the Hall and the brick floor of the Parlour

Top Arch brace in the Hall

Middle Wattle and daub

Bottom Oak beams around the front door

The house as a home

Little is known about the original occupants of the house.

In 1395–6 the advowson (the right to nominate a person to be parish priest) was acquired by Michelham Priory in Hailsham, though the Bishop of Chichester stipulated that a portion of the rectory of Alfriston must be for 'the keep of a vicar or perpetual chaplain, who shall reside in person'. It is impossible to know whether that referred to the Clergy House; although it remained church property for the next five centuries, it was not a vicarage in the modern sense of the term. When not occupied by a vicar, it was let as a source of income for the church.

Below Numerous postcards have been made of the Clergy House; the north front before the start of restoration work

Old Parsonage, Alfriston.
Before Restoration. 084.

After Michelham Priory was dissolved in 1538, the advowson was briefly held by Sir Thomas Cromwell and then by Anne of Cleves. The mid-16th-century work on the Clergy House may have been to adapt the house for occupation by a married vicar and his family or lease as a family home.

The first recorded vicar with a family was Hugh Walker who was appointed to the living in 1593; he had seven children who were baptised at St Andrew's, and possibly four more christened elsewhere. Probably the last vicar to live in the Clergy House was the unmarried Rev. Robert North who was vicar from 1671 to 1709 and had to appear before the ecclesiastical authorities for negligence in his duties and to confess 'some excess in drinking … at his house in Alfriston'.

Alfriston was not a good living. Though elevated to a market town in 1405 and a trading centre in the 15th century, its prosperity was short-lived and by the 17th century it was 'a decayed commercial centre'. Moreover a considerable number of dissenters lived there. After North's time, vicars were often absentees living in Lewes or Seaford and there were vacancies as long as five years.

Multiple occupancy

The Clergy House's decline during the 19th century is reflected in the 1841 census which shows 11 people living in the house: Robert Foord, an agricultural labourer, his wife Florence and their four children; John Coates, a labourer, his wife Harriet and their daughter Barbara; Walter Herbert, no occupation given; and Joseph Lower, bargemaster. He was a descendant of John Lower who died in 1801 and was, according to his tomb, 'the first person who navigated the Cuckmere River to Alfriston'.

The 1861 census reveals two families still living in the house: John and Harriet Coates remained with their lodger, Joseph Lower. The new additions were the Aukett family: George Aukett, an agricultural labourer and groom, and his wife Susannah with their seven children.

By the time of the 1881 census, only Harriet Coates, then 80, remained as the sole resident, described as a widow. The address had become The Old Vicarage. Harriet had married in 1817 and become a laundress and a bell-ringer at St Andrew's, and it was she who pleaded with Beynon's predecessor to be allowed to remain in the house until her death.

Above A pane scratched with the name of E. Lower, 3 or 31 July (?) 1891 when no one was living in the house. The glass has been etched from the outside

Left This summer view shows the extensive climbing plants that once covered much of the north front

'Preserve from decay'

Some work had been carried out for the Rev. Beynon before the National Trust acquired the Clergy House.

Using the £225 9s 6d Beynon succeeded in raising between 1889 and June 1896, Owen Fleming used a non-local firm to board the roof, but the first Secretary of the SPAB, Hugh Thackeray Turner, reported to Beynon that the boarding was of poor quality. Nor was Owen Fleming willing to meet someone from the SPAB, perhaps anticipating the society's likely view on his suggestion for a minstrels' gallery.

Records of the first work carried out on a National Trust building are scant. It would appear that Alfred Powell's estimates had been optimistic as in May 1896 he asked Thackeray Turner 'to explain to the NT the impossibility of accurate previous estimation of cost in such works', and the following month an appeal letter appeared in the *Standard* stating £855 was needed.

'We should, very naturally, be asked to "restore" it, in so far as that odious word means preserve from decay...'

Octavia Hill, 16 February 1895

THE OLD CLERGY HOUSE, ALFRISTON. 8631

Left The Clergy House after its first re-thatching under the National Trust

OLD CLEREY HOUSE ALFRISTON

Sufficient funds were raised for the work to be carried out, presumably before it was first occupied in September 1898. The rear wall had to be rebuilt, and the fireplace and upper floor within the Hall were removed to restore its original appearance. A floor of chalk and sour milk was reinstated, and the roof was rethatched with Norfolk water reed.

In the early 1930s S.P.B. Mais, while researching a walking book and passing through Alfriston, 'found men hard at work re-thatching its steeply pitched roof. A … young man told me that the reeds all came from Norfolk and were becoming increasingly difficult to procure, and that he and his mates, who came from Cambridgeshire, were so much in demand for this nearly lost art that they would have to go straight on from Alfriston to Birkenhead.'

Powell and the SPAB were again involved with repairs in 1938 in response to a beetle infestation.

Above A rather unsightly fence has been erected to screen the garden, perhaps while today's hedge grew

The Society for the Protection of Ancient Buildings

The SPAB was founded in 1877 by the artist, writer and campaigner William Morris and architect Philip Webb to counter the needless destruction and damaging alteration of historic buildings. Morris and Webb drew up the Society's manifesto, setting out its distinctive approach to the repair and care of old buildings, which still guides the SPAB's work today. The early SPAB was, therefore, well placed to give advice and support to the National Trust in the acquisition and renovation of its first building. A representative of the SPAB still sits on the National Trust Council.

A Tenanted House

There were no complaints about the Clergy House's condition in letters written from the building when it was used by the Arts and Crafts designer and entrepreneur C.R. Ashbee and his wife Janet Forbes for their honeymoon in September 1898.

Ashbee knew of the building because he had become a member of the National Trust Council in July 1896 and would follow Rawnsley in making a fundraising tour of the United States in 1900.

The Ashbees bathed in the river and Janet, then aged 20, wrote a postscript to a letter from Ashbee to his 'dear little mother' that:

> we have arranged a highly decorative and sweet-scented frieze of red cheeked apples round the beams which intersect our diningroom – they look just <u>lovely</u>!'

Below The River Cuckmere from the garden

Daringly for the time, Janet took off her stays by the river and never wore them again. Ashbee reported to his mother that:

> … The 'honey-moon' so far has been a great success, much more so than I expected – because we spend it in a rational way. We pursue the [?]fast method of life. Breakfast at 8 or 7.45, and then spend the first 2 hours of the morning writing our letters of which there are [?] to send, and reading. At about 11.30 we pack up books and lunch on to our bicycles and start off for a bathe, to a lonely cove under the chalk cliffs about 5 miles away. After bathing we lunch, spend the afternoon in reading and ride home again in time for dinner at about 7 or 7.30. After that we read again and so to bed.

Ashbee stayed at the Clergy House again at Easter 1900 with members of his Guild of Handicraft, which he had founded in 1888. His 1900 journal refers to 'a fine roaring party this year at Alfriston, eleven of us, and all in holiday humour.'

Rather perplexingly the National Trust report for 1898 records that 'a responsible tenant has been found for each of the two cottages into which the building is divided'. It seems that the Trust had let the house to the writers Lionel Curtis and Max Balfour, since it was they who made it available to the Ashbees.

If the sequence and even identity of early tenants are in doubt, there is none about the longest lease, assigned to Robert Witt.

Opposite C.R. Ashbee by the Scottish painter and engraver William Strang (1859–1921), perhaps best-known for his 1918 portrait of Vita Sackville-West, *Lady with a Red Hat*

Bottom Ashbee's wife, Janet Forbes (1878–1961), also by William Strang. She was the daughter of a wealthy London stockbroker

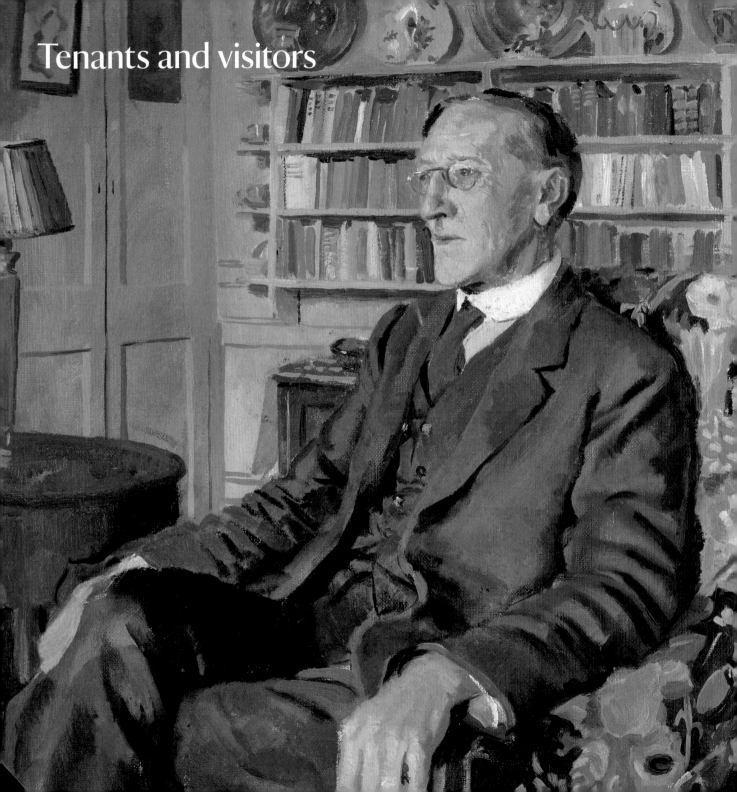

By far the longest and most illustrious of the National Trust's tenants was Robert Witt (1872–1952). He had admired the house when a student and had taken a tenancy by the early years of the 20th century, using the house as a weekend retreat from London until 1940.

After studying history at Oxford, Witt served in the army during the Matabele uprising and was a war correspondent alongside Cecil Rhodes. On his return to England he qualified as a solicitor, rising to become senior partner in one of London's most prominent law firms.

His passion for art inspired his first book, published in 1902, entitled *How to Look at Pictures*. The following year he co-founded the National Art-Collections Fund (now the Art Fund), becoming its first honorary Secretary and then Chairman until 1945, when he was made the NA-CF's first President. He was also a trustee of the National, Tate and Watts galleries, and in 1932 he co-founded the

Courtauld Institute of Art, bequeathing to it the colossal collection of photographs and prints of paintings – said at the time to be the largest in the world – which he and his wife, Mary Helene Marten, had built up. Witt helped Helen Frick to establish a comparable resource in the United States, the Frick Art Reference Library.

Until the 1930s the tenancy of the Clergy House was shared with Charles Aitken (1869–1936); they may have met at New College, Oxford, but they would have worked together even before Aitken's appointment as Director of the Tate Gallery. He possessed the odd faculty of automatic drawing, and at the Clergy House his output took medieval form. To counter the unfortunate impulse of visitors to write their name on the walls, Aitken put up a notice: 'Please refrain from writing your name on the walls. A book is provided.'

From 1948 the tenants were Misses Greyke-Clarke and Lavauden; only the Hall was open to visitors. In 1974 the tenancy ended, and the decision was taken to open most of the house to visitors.

Above Sir Robert Witt by Sir Oswald Birley (1880–1952), 1931. Birley painted several portraits of Sir Winston Churchill, to whom he gave painting lessons

Left The Bone family and Isobel Dacre, a well-known English artist and suffragette, by Francis Dodd (1874–1949). Dodd was an official war artist and a trustee of the Tate Gallery, who stayed at the Clergy House at the invitation of the Witts

Opposite Charles Aitken by Stephen Bone (1904–58), c.1932. Aitken became the Tate Gallery's first Director, from 1917 to 1930, and this portrait was presented to the gallery by Sir Robert and Lady Witt. © Estate of Stephen Bone. All Rights Reserved, DACS 2017

The Interior

Visitors enter the house through the garden door at the back of the building, which leads into a small room in the mid-18th-century lean-to.

In the far left-hand corner is an exposed section of the original outside wall showing the wattle and daub infill. The laths were split rather than sawn and woven when still green, a technique still used for fencing panels today. Beyond it is the oven. The steps opposite the door lead into the mid-16th-century west wing.

Above The medieval oakleaf carving in the Hall

Right The ogee-headed doorways off the Hall

Opposite The hearth in the centre of the Hall

The Parlour

This became the principal family room of the house in the 16th century, made out of the two previous service rooms, the pantry and the buttery, indicated by the two surviving openings on to the Hall. A staircase against the south wall would have led to the rooms above, which served either as storage space or servants' quarters, probably until the 'best end' was swapped over in the mid-16th century.

In the left-hand corner of the fireplace is the bread oven. After this had been heated with faggots, dough would be placed inside with a peel, a long-handled shovel made out of wood or iron. The furniture is all 17th-century and made of English oak, apart from a pair of benches, which are chestnut and probably French.

The Hall

The ground-floor open hall has a long tradition in England, stretching back to Saxon times and surviving into the 17th century in many parts of the Weald. The communal centre of the building was where the unmarried vicar or family would have eaten, sitting on a bench at the well-lit east end of the Hall. It again rises through two storeys to the rafters, but the positions of the joists that supported the upper floor, removed in 1896, can still be seen. The roof is supported on timbers that incorporate a central vertical 'crown-post', which gives its name to this kind of construction. The crossbeams that form the inner walls at the east and west ends are elaborately moulded, and in the north-east corner the point at which they meet is carved in the form of an oak leaf. It has been suggested that this may have inspired the National Trust symbol, but unfortunately no evidence has been found to support the idea.

Remains of the original hearth were discovered in the centre of the room during the 1970s archaeological work, and smoke-blackened roof timbers can still be seen.

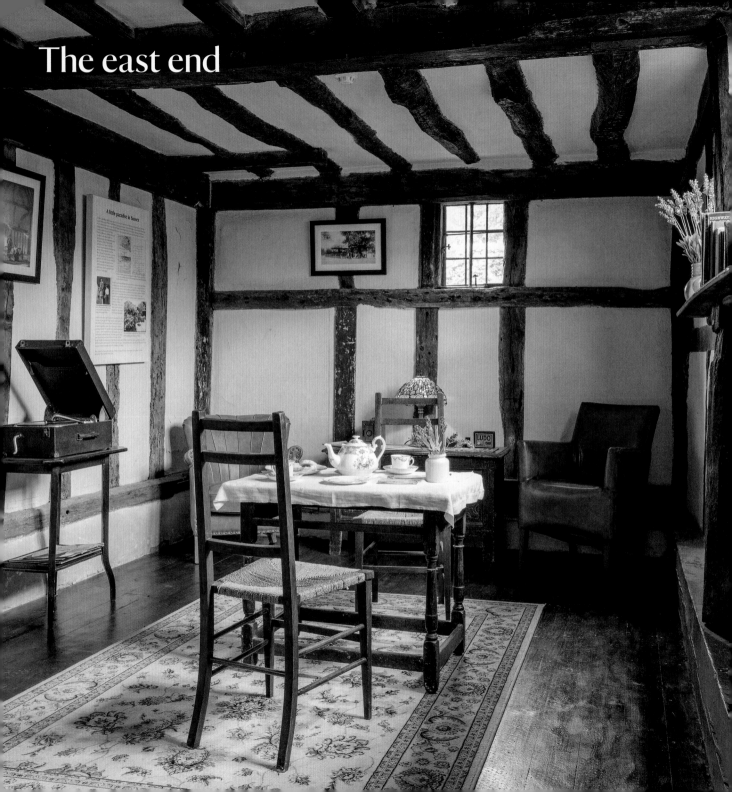

A little paradise in Sussex

Opposite The 1920s-themed Reading Room

Below The Victorian Bedroom with its small fireplace and door to the staircase on the left. The room is used to tell the story behind the saving of the house

This was originally the end of the house occupied by the family rooms until the mid-16th century when the alterations transposed family and servant ends.

Reading Room

When the house was built in the Middle Ages, this room was used as the family living room. A door towards the southern end of the west wall originally provided access from the Hall before construction of the lean-to passage. A staircase in the south-west corner provided access to the family bedroom above. The date the cast-iron stove was installed is unknown. It is called the Reading Room today to acknowledge Rev. Beynon's idea to make the room a 'reading room', somewhere for the villagers to meet, write and read, and has been dressed to reflect this purpose.

Today the room is used to tell the story of the contribution made by the Witts' tenancy to the garden in particular; its appearance today owes much to the work they carried out.

The Bedroom

Prior to the mid-16th-century alterations, this room was the solar, which was used as the family's bed- and sitting-room. Today it is dressed as the late 19th-century bedroom of Harriet Coates, the last tenant of the Clergy House before the Trust bought it, though it is not certain that she did use it as such. It now contains an exhibition telling the story of the house and the part she, the Rev. Beynon and the National Trust played in saving the house.

The Garden and Wildlife

The garden is bordered by the River Cuckmere, which rises near Heathfield and reaches the English Channel at Cuckmere Haven. Though small, its mix of formal planting, orchard, kitchen garden and wilder areas make it a haven for wildlife.

The garden covers about a quarter of a hectare, and the thin layer of poor alkaline topsoil lies on chalk, which makes it quite a challenge to grow anything successfully. The layout owes much to Sir Robert and Lady Witt who terraced what was a rather daunting slope towards the river and created the brickwork and paths and the garden 'rooms'. Their intention was to create a typical Edwardian summer garden, and the National Trust has continued that vision with some refinements by Graham Stuart Thomas, who became garden adviser to the National Trust from 1955 to 1975 after an earlier informal association. We know few details of the Witts' planting, but they brought the large amphora, seen on the Judas tree lawn and in the herb and rose gardens, from their travels in Crete and Morocco.

The garden is a challenge in that part of it is often flooded by the Cuckmere for three months of the year. This is a relatively new phenomenon, as the Witts were able to row on the river before it silted up. Yew hedges and a

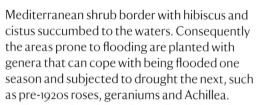

Below left Looking east from the vegetable garden; the self-seeded poppies help attract pollinators

Clockwise from top A terracotta amphora collected by Sir Robert and Lady Witt; a lead cistern of 1788 in the herb garden; snake's head fritillaries enjoy the damp end of the orchard, which is regularly flooded in winter; large-flowered tulips are planted in the borders to stand out against emerging summer-flowering perennials and roses; pots of tulips add colour to the steps at the rear of the house

Mediterranean shrub border with hibiscus and cistus succumbed to the waters. Consequently the areas prone to flooding are planted with genera that can cope with being flooded one season and subjected to drought the next, such as pre-1920s roses, geraniums and Achillea.

The roses have been chosen for their perfume and are a mix of albas, gallicas, bourbons, rugosas and hybrid musks. They have been underplanted with campanulas, herbaceous geraniums and other cottage garden favourites. Spring bulbs provide interest early in the year.

The Box Garden
The Box Tree Garden is a medieval-style square garden bounded by yew hedges and divided by paths. The clipped box trees are underplanted with old laced pinks. At its centre is a sundial, commissioned to mark the centenary of the National Trust in 1995, sitting on a balustrade of London's old Waterloo Bridge which was designed by John Rennie and opened in 1817.

The Herb Garden
This garden to the west of the house contains mostly flowering herbs used in medieval times for medicinal purposes. Many of the plants are mentioned in Nicholas Culpepper's *Complete Herbal* of 1653: bugle (*Ajuga reptans*) was used to stem internal bleeding and for throat infections; bistort (*Persicaria bistorta*) was used as an astringent; lungwort (*Pulmonaria officinalis*) helped with lung disorders; and devil's bit scabious (*Succisa pratensis*) was used to treat fevers, poisoning and plague.

The Vegetable Garden and Orchard

The Vegetable Garden is run without the use of pesticides, so there is a focus on growing the more reliable and resilient vegetables throughout the year.

Railway sleepers edge the eight raised beds: four of them are planted with annual favourites including potatoes, runner beans, beetroot, courgettes, carrots and leeks; the other four beds are used to grow perennial vegetables such as rhubarb and globe artichokes and as a plant nursery area. The raised beds are surrounded by narrow borders containing a mixture of herbs and flowering plants such as lemon balm, lavender, mint, English marigold and poppies.

The Orchard

This is the only part of the garden that predates the National Trust, as confirmed by Octavia Hill's 1896 description of the Clergy House as 'tiny but beautiful, with Orchard and a sweep of lowland river behind it'. In front of the orchard is the Judas tree (*Cercis siliquastrum*), so called because it is a tree of this Mediterranean species from which Judas Iscariot is believed to have hanged himself. It was damaged in the hurricane-force winds of 1987 and has shown signs of being in decline in recent years. However, a programme of pollarding to rejuvenate the tree and stimulate fresh growth, as well as ongoing propagation attempts, should ensure its continued survival, and it still produces a good show of pink flowers in early June, which are traditionally said to resemble drops of blood.

Most of the trees were lost in the 1987 storm, and the Orchard was replanted with old and rare apple varieties such as Sussex Duck's Bill, Charles Ross, Monarch, Lady Sudeley, Crawley Beauty and the local Alfriston Apple. They are a mixture of culinary and dessert apples. The apple trees tend to lean over, as their weakened roots cannot support their weight.

Other notable trees in the orchard include a mulberry (*Morus nigra*), which produces edible black fruits in September, and a medlar (*Mespilus germanica*), the fruits of which are usually made into a jelly.

The grass is cut as a hay meadow and is home to some important spring wild flowers.

Opposite above When the apples ripen in summer, buttercups take centre stage

Opposite below The Orchard at blossom time in spring. Among the spring flowers are fritillaria, daffodils and winter heliotrope

Left The productive Vegetable Garden with sweetcorn, beans, sweet peas and carrots

A haven for wildlife

In spring the garden starts to come alive with the sound of birdsong. Reed warblers and reed bunting can be heard calling from the river, and a pair of moorhens makes a nest amongst the reeds.

Blue tits feed on tiny insects and often make use of the nest boxes hung around the garden to raise their young. Tiny holly blues, often the first butterflies to emerge in the new year, feed from the pollen-rich flowers of the ivy that clambers over the ageing flint walls. Hummingbird hawk-moths dart amongst the flowers of the buddleia near the entrance, drinking nectar with their specially adapted tongues. The characteristic laugh of the green woodpecker echoes through the garden. This colourful bird is a welcome visitor as they often feed on the larvae of beetles that might otherwise destroy the delicate root systems of the garden plants and flowers.

Summer is an excellent time to watch out for dragonflies and damselflies over the river and reed bed. Banded demoiselles are particularly stunning, with smoky patches in the middle of their wings a contrast to the metallic green and blue of their bodies. Ruddy darters sit perfectly still on waterside leaves and stems as they watch for their prey of small airborne insects. The majestic blue and green emperor, the largest of our native dragonflies, patrols up and down as it seeks out unsuspecting insects to devour with its powerful jaws.

Left Natterer's bats (*Myotis nattereri*) roost in the open space of the Clergy House Hall with the main access point a timber at the front of the building

The Clergy House also welcomes a fabulous array of mammals in the summer. The thatched roof becomes a home for a nursery roost of natterer's bats, whilst brown long-eared bats fly slowly through the trees as they hunt for tiny moths and other airborne insects. Unlike most other bats, they use their eyesight to hunt for prey and so can sometimes be spotted flying during the day as well as at dusk. Field voles and shrews scurry through the kitchen garden, and make a tasty meal for tawny owls watching with keen eyes from the trees above. On quieter days the dark flash of a mink can be seen near the reeds as they hunt for rabbits, one of their favourite foods.

Autumn sees gathering flocks of swallows and house martins stopping off to feed before their long journey south to sub-Saharan Africa where they will overwinter. Conkers fall from the spreading branches of the horse chestnut tree, and the roses are laden with ripe hips. The bright cobalt flash of a kingfisher can still be spotted to brighten up a grey day as the garden begins to tuck itself up for the coming winter.

Far left The majestic Green woodpecker (*Picus viridis*) is often seen in early morning feeding on the Judas tree lawn

Left The delicate Banded demoiselle damselfly (*Calopteryx splendens*) darts up and down the water beside the garden

Opposite, top Male holly blue butterfly (*Celastrina argiolus*), which can be found feeding in the garden

Opposite, bottom The stunning hummingbird hawk-moth (*Macroglossum stellatarum*) can be seen enjoying the red valerian by the Judas tree lawn

The Clergy House's Setting

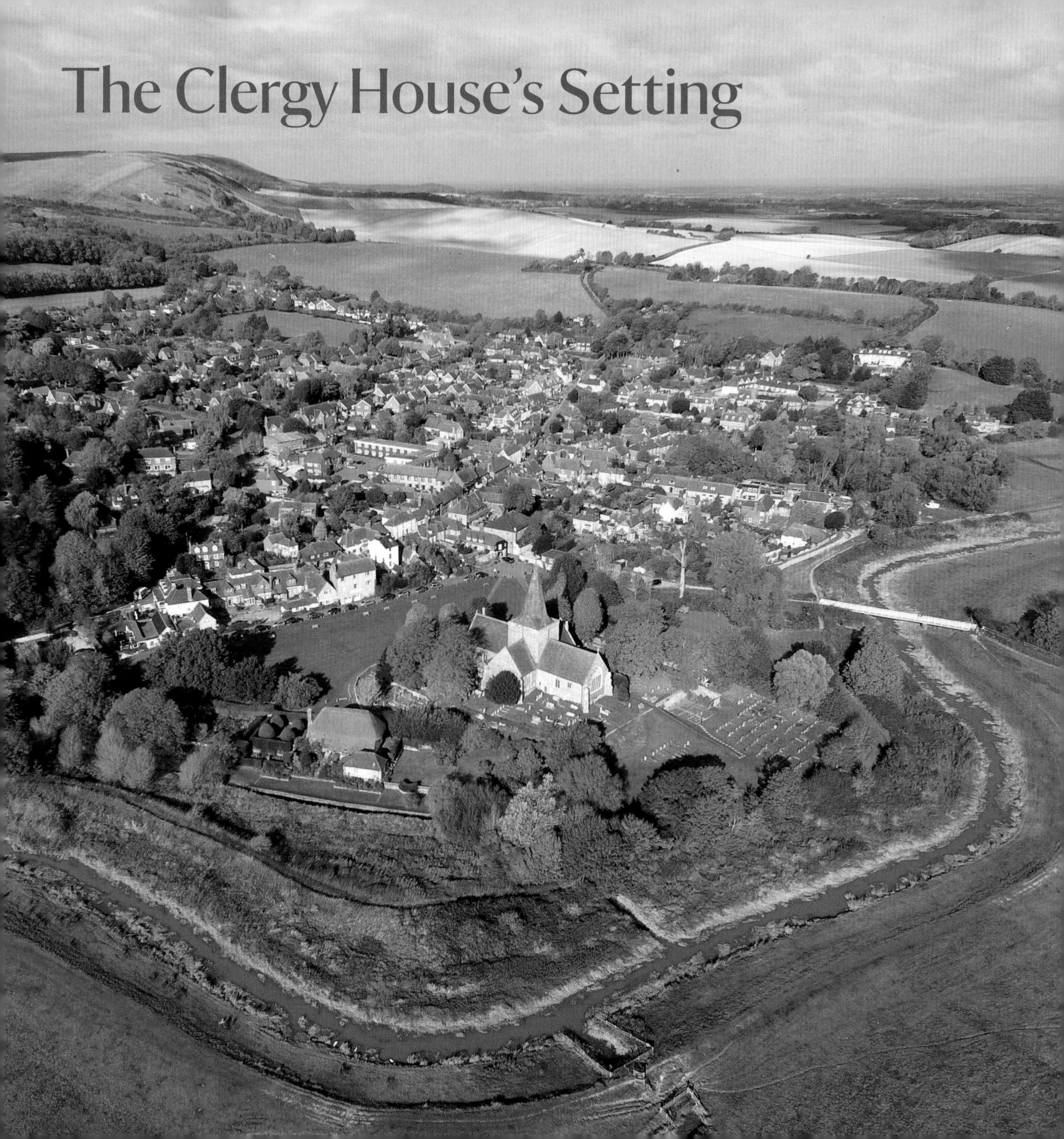

The Wealden village of Alfriston lies in the Cuckmere Valley nestled below the South Downs. It is likely that the surrounding area was occupied from neolithic times as large numbers of prehistoric barrows are still evident higher up in the surrounding downland.

In Saxon times the village was recorded as Aelfrictun (the town of Alfric), from which the Domesday Book records the town as 'Elfricesh-tun'. During the Napoleonic Wars, large numbers of troops were billeted in Alfriston in case the invaders got past the Martello towers along the Channel coast. As a result the village thrived with locals providing food, drink and many other services to the troops. When the Napoleonic Wars ended, many of the villagers turned to smuggling to make ends meet. The notoriously violent Alfriston gang used the Cuckmere river to bring their illegally landed goods into the village ready for distribution inland. The gang broke apart after its leader, a butcher named Stanton Collins who lived in what is now Smugglers' Inn, was sentenced in 1831 at the Sussex Winter Assizes in Lewes for stealing barley, and sentenced to seven years' transportation to Van Diemen's Land (Tasmania).

The streets of Alfriston are a harmonious patchwork of historic buildings from half a dozen centuries, with three remaining pubs – the Star Inn, the George Inn and the Smugglers. The Star was originally a religious hostel built in 1345 and used to accommodate monks and pilgrims en route from Battle Abbey to the shrine of St Richard, patron saint of Sussex, at Chichester Cathedral. Wooden figures decorate the upper part of the building, while at the front is a one-time ship's figurehead representing a red lion. The latter is connected with the Alfriston smuggling gang who used the inn as a base.

A conical lock-up that probably once housed smugglers can still be seen in the car park to the north west of the village.

Many of the old buildings here are still tiled in Horsham slate, created from Sussex Wealden sandstone and used for roofing on more prestigious buildings since Roman times. It is thought that the Clergy House was also roofed with it.

In 1931 Eleanor Farjeon wrote the popular hymn 'Morning Has Broken' in Alfriston, supposedly inspired by the beauty she saw around the village.

Left The Clergy House, visitor centre building and St Andrew's, seen from across the River Cuckmere

Top The River Cuckmere and Alfriston village

Above The Clergy House and the 'Cathedral of the Downs' are depicted on the village sign

Opposite Alfriston village with the Clergy House and National Trust visitor reception building in the foreground

St Andrew's Church

On a mound in the village green known as the Tye stands the fine 14th-century church of St Andrew's known as the 'Cathedral of the Downs'. Almost certainly funded largely by the wool trade, it was founded c.1360, before the Clergy House was built.

It is built on the remains of a large Saxon burial mound and on what is thought to be the site of a smaller church. That earlier church may have been the burial place of St Lewinna, a virgin martyr killed in 690 by heathen Saxons – Sussex was the last Saxon county to be converted to Christianity, in the 8th century. Her relics later attracted so much veneration that a visiting Flemish Benedictine monk named Balgerus stole them from a church dedicated to St Andrew and spirited them away to the Abbey of St Winoc at Bergues in northern France in 1058. However, Beddingham, Bishopstone, Jevington and Lewes also have churches dedicated to St Andrew, and there is no mention of a church at Alfriston in the Domesday Book.

It remains a mystery why such a grand and remarkable building should have been built for a village of a few hundred people. Built in the form of a Greek cross, the church displays exceptional workmanship. Carefully chosen flints have been knapped square to minimise the use of mortar, and greensand stone has been used for quoins, buttresses and facings. Like many buildings in the village, the church's king-post roof was once covered in Horsham stone-slates, but the stones have been replaced by clay tiles to reduce the weight. The square tower rises above the crossing, its broach spire now clad with chestnut shingles.

The piers of the arches into the nave, chancel and transepts are semi-octagonal and fluted. A remnant of the murals that once covered the walls can be seen on the north side of the altar. The sanctuary contains two finely carved features: in the north wall is the Easter Sepulchre, its ogee canopy ending in corbels depicting a woman's face and a curled-up dog with head between its hind legs. On the slab stand statues saved from the demolition of the reredos in 1987: St Aphege, Archbishop of Canterbury from 1006, and St Andrew flank a scene in which Jesus calls Andrew from his nets to become a 'fisher of men'.

Opposite, in the south wall, is a sedilla where three assistants at holy communion could sit. Its trefoil, as those of the piscina and sepulchre, is the same design as that at the end of the principal beam of the Old Clergy House.

Opposite St Andrew's from the west. The church contains stained glass by Charles Eamer Kempe whose principal country-house commission was Wightwick Manor near Wolverhampton (also National Trust)

Left St Andrew's and its south transept from the Clergy House orchard

The South Downs and Cuckmere Valley

The South Downs are a chalk landscape of rolling hills risen from the sea, of glorious heathland, river valleys, ancient woodland, thriving villages and market towns, and the white cliffs of the Heritage Coast, genuinely iconic.

The South Downs is Britain's newest National Park and are relatively unpopulated compared to the rest of the south east, although in Sussex there are large urban seaside resorts, including Brighton, Hove and Eastbourne.

The continual erosion of vulnerable landscapes through road building and development has prompted the National Trust to focus on acquiring ancient escarpment landscapes. It is no coincidence that during the First World War the chalk country of southern England and the South Downs in particular was used to foster a sense of emotional attachment that would motivate and sustain a nation at arms. The Trust's holding of these fragile downland landscapes – Kipling's 'whale-backed Downs' – is now substantial, and they are managed to enhance the botanically rich, close-cropped turf by sheep grazing.

The South Downs contain a glorious and diverse mix of habitats. Mixed and ancient woodlands support many specialist species such as the rare barbastelle bat and our native bluebell. Chyngton Farm on the west side of the Cuckmere estuary has exceptional wetland habitats such as wet pasture meadows and relict salt-marsh; in winter they support lapwing, wigeon and teal which can be seen feeding alongside waders such as ringed and grey plovers, redshank and curlew.

The heathlands, though only small in area, are home to an array of distinctive plant and animal communities and heathland specialists such as the tiny silver-studded blue butterfly. Species-rich chalk grassland can be found in the Cradle Valley, which attracts rare butterflies.

The coastal habitats of the chalk cliffs and salt-marsh at the eastern end of the downs see seabirds such as nesting kittiwakes and fulmars, and the internationally rare vegetated shingle beaches are home to yellow horned-poppy and sea kale. Well-managed farmland provides flower-rich meadows, arable land and hedgerows which all provide important homes for rare and threatened plants and wildlife such as the grey partridge and beautiful corn marigold.

Below Sunset reflected in a meander of the River Cuckmere

Clockwise from top left Lapwing with its splendid crest; sea kale (*Crambe maritima*); common ringed plover (*Charadrius hiaticula*), one of the prettiest wading birds; the view over the River Cuckmere from the rear of the Clergy House; hay bales on Chyngton Farm with the Seven Sisters in the distance; a fulmar (*Fulmarius glacialis*) turning along a cliff edge